Be An Expert!™

Pets

Erin Kelly

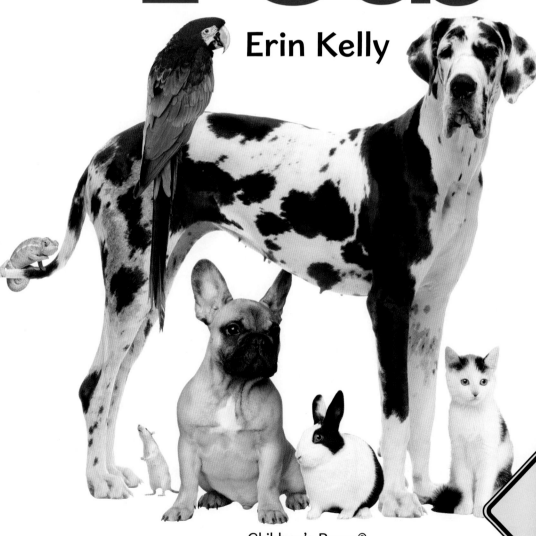

Children's Press®
An imprint of Scholastic Inc.

Contents

Know the Names

Be an expert! Get to know the names of these pets.

Dogs

They are our friends!

Zoom In

Find these parts in the big picture.

snout   **fur**   **paws**   **tail**

Birds

Some can talk!

little corella

parrot

cockatiel

canary

budgie

Expert Fact

Talking birds don't understand what they are saying. They **mimic** sounds they hear.

Cats

They purr.

Pet Smarts

Q: What does it mean when a cat's tail gets very **bushy**?

A: It usually means that the cat is scared.

Fish

See them swim in the fish tank!

neon tetra fish

guppy fish

oscar
fish

zebra danio fish

molly fish

guppy fish

Zoom In

Find these parts in the big picture.

| eye | gill | dorsal fin | tail fin |

Guinea Pigs

They love kids!

Expert Fact

When guinea pigs are happy, they jump straight up in the air! This is called popcorning.

Lizards

They like to climb.

green
anole

panther
chameleons

African fat-tailed gecko

standing's day gecko

Pet Smarts

Q: What does a lizard do when a **predator** grabs its tail?

A: Most lizards can separate their tails from their bodies to run away. They will grow a new tail!

bearded dragon

Rabbits

Their noses are a little wet.
They are also cute!

Zoom In

Find these parts in the big picture.

nose

ears

whiskers

foot

Turtles

They have shells!

Expert Fact

Some turtles grow to be as big as a garbage can lid! They need an **aquarium** that fits them.

All the Pets

They are lovable.
Thanks, pets!

1.

2.

5.

6.

Expert Quiz

Do you know the names of these pets? Then you are an expert! See if someone else can name them too!

3.

4.

7.

8.

Answers: 1. Bird. 2. Fish. 3. Lizard. 4. Dog. 5. Rabbits. 6. Turtle. 7. Guinea pig. 8. Cats.

21

Expert Gear

Meet a veterinarian, a doctor for animals. What does she need to keep pets healthy?

She has **scrubs**.

She has a **stethoscope**.

She has **gloves**.

She has **scissors**.

Glossary

aquarium (uh-KWAIR-ee-uhm): a glass tank in which you can keep fish or other animals.

bushy (BUSH-ee): thick and spreading.

mimic (MIM-ik): to imitate someone.

Hello!

predator (PRED-uh-tur): an animal that lives by hunting other animals for food.

Index

Library of Congress Cataloging-in-Publication Data
Names: Kelly, Erin Suzanne, 1965- author.
Title: Pets/Erin Kelly. Other titles: Be an expert! (Scholastic Inc.)
Description: New York: Children's Press, an imprint of Scholastic, 2021. |Series: Be an expert! | Includes index. | Audience: Ages 4-5. | Audience: Grades K-1. | Summary: "Book introduces the reader to different pets"—Provided by publisher.
Identifiers: LCCN 2020002690 | ISBN 9780531130544 (library binding) | ISBN 9780531131596 (paperback)
Subjects: LCSH: Pets—Juvenile literature.
Classification: LCC SF416.2 .K45 2021 | DDC 636.088/7—dc23
LC record available at https://lccn.loc.gov/2020002690

Printed in Heshan, China 62

SCHOLASTIC, CHILDREN'S PRESS, BE AN EXPERT!™, and associated logos are trademarks and/or registered trademarks of Scholastic Inc.

2 3 4 5 6 7 8 9 10 R 30 29 28 27 26 25 24 23 22 21

Scholastic Inc., 557 Broadway, New York, NY 10012.

Art direction and design by THREE DOGS DESIGN LLC.

Photos ©: back cover: Mark Taylor/Minden Pictures; 2: yellowsarah/Getty Images; 3 top left: 101cats/Getty Images; 3 center right: Mark Taylor/Minden Pictures; 6 bottom right: yellowsarah/Getty Images; 7 bottom right: vitalssss/Getty Images; 8 center: 101cats/Getty Images; 8 bottom left: Viorika/Getty Images; 9 inset bottom: Sonsedska/Getty Images; 9 top right: Waitforlight/Getty Images; 13 top: Juniors Bildarchiv GmbH/Alamy Images; 16 right: Petra Wegner/Nature Picture Library; 17 bottom: Mark Taylor/Minden Pictures; 20 center left: yellowsarah/Getty Images; 20 bottom left: Mark Taylor/Minden Pictures; 21 bottom right: 101cats/Getty Images; 22: West Coast Surfer/age fotostock; 23 center top: Waitforlight/Getty Images.

All other photos © Shutterstock.

Front cover: A group of domestic pets. **Back cover:** A rabbit with its baby.